Feasts & Seasons

Winter

Feasts & Seasons

Winter

Anthony Adams
Robert Leach
Roy Palmer

BLACKIE

BLACKIE & SON LTD
Bishopbriggs, Glasgow G64 2NZ
450 Edgware Road, London W2 1EG

Printed in Great Britain by Robert MacLehose & Co. Ltd
Printers to the University of Glasgow

Contents

Acknowledgments

The authors and publishers are grateful for permission to use copyright material as follows:

Oxford University Press for the extracts from *The Lore and Language of Schoolchildren* by Iona and Peter Opie.

B.B.C. for the song, "Black, White, Yellow and Green".

The Director, School of Scottish Studies, University of Edinburgh, for the recipe (p 31) from *Tocher* which was taken from the R. C. Maclagan MSS.

The National Museum of Wales (Welsh Folk Museum) for the songs "Cân y Fari Lwyd" and "Cân y Grempog" from *Caneuon Llafar Gwlad* (vol. 1) ed. by D. Roy Saer.

The Reader's Digest Association Ltd for the recipe (p 38) from *The Cookery Year*.

David Higham Associates Limited for the extract and verse from *The English Festivals* by Laurence Whistler, published by Heinemann, 1947.

E.F.D.S. Publications Ltd (Chappell & Co. Ltd) for "Valentine Chant" from the album *Green Groves*; collected by Fred Hamer; copyright E.F.D.S. Publications Ltd.

William Heinemann Ltd for the song, "Dame Durden" from *A Song for Every Season* by Bob Copper.

John Johnson, Authors' Agent, for "Death of a Bird in January" by Philip Callow.

Crispin Gill, editor of *The Countryman*, for "The Bullfinch" by Betty Hughes from *The Countryman*.

Frederick Warne & Co. Ltd for the extracts from *A Year of Festivals* by Geoffrey Palmer and Noel Lloyd.

Dr Leslie Paul for the extract from *The Boy Down Kitchener Street*, published by Faber and Faber.

The Trustees of the Hardy Estate and Macmillan, London and Basingstoke, for "Snow in the Suburbs" from *Collected Poems* by Thomas Hardy.

Illustrations
Rev. Canon G. R. Fishley   Page 4
The Mansell Collection   pages 6, 7 (top), 20, 42, 46, 51 and 52.
Leslie Shepard for the carol sheet from *The History of Street Literature*   page 8.
William Heinemann Ltd for the woodcuts from *The English Festivals* by Laurence Whistler   page 13.
Illustrated London News   pages 21 and 37.
The Mander and Mitchenson Theatre Collection   page 27.
The National Museum of Wales (Welsh Folk Museum)   pages 28 and 32.
Bibliothèque Nationale, Paris   page 36.
J. D. Owen, Curator, Ceredigion Museum, Aberystwyth, for the wassail bowl (property of University College of Wales, Aberystwyth).
The Victoria and Albert Museum   page 40.
The Post Office   page 43
The Birmingham Post & Mail Ltd   page 50.
Preston North End F.C. Ltd   page 53.

Songs
A special acknowledgment is due to Pat Palmer for the harmonization of songs, and notes on their performance.

When Icicles Hang by the Wall

When icicles hang by the wall,
  And Dick the shepherd blows his nail,
And Tom bears logs into the hall,
  And milk comes frozen home in pail;
When blood is nipped, and ways be foul,
Then nightly sings the staring owl,
                Tu-who;
  Tu-whit, tu-who – a merry note,
  While greasy Joan doth keel the pot.

When all aloud the wind doth blow,
  And coughing drowns the parson's saw,
And birds sit brooding in the snow,
  And Marian's nose looks red and raw,
When roasted crabs hiss in the bowl,
Then nightly sings the staring owl,
                Tu-who;
  Tu-whit, tu-who – a merry note,
  While greasy Joan doth keel the pot.

William Shakespeare

The Twilight of the Gods
(How Winter Came)

Odin was the most powerful of the gods of Asgard. But Baldur, his son, was the best loved. He was so bright and handsome that he was called Baldur the Beautiful.

But he had bad dreams. He dreamed of dying.

So his mother, Frigga, made everything on earth promise not to harm him. He was safe from water, fire, stone, iron, disease, poison, birds, wild animals and cruel reptiles. Nothing could harm him.

The gods celebrated his certain safety. They tried to hurt him, but the swords they struck with and the missiles they hurled simply bounced off him. Everyone laughed, certain that Baldur the Beautiful was safe from death.

But Loki, cunning, jealous, meddlesome Loki, saw his brother gods at this sport, and a great evil swelled up in his heart. He disguised himself as a silly old woman and went to Frigga, Baldur's mother.

"Why isn't he hurt?" Loki asked, pointing.

"Because he can't be hurt," answered Frigga light-heartedly. "Because everything on earth has sworn never to hurt him."

"Everything?" said Loki meanly.

"Well – there's the mistletoe bush," said Frigga. "But it was so small I didn't bother with it."

Loki chuckled to himself. He went and found a mistletoe bush, and broke off a branch. This he fashioned into a sharp-pointed dart. Then he went back to where the gods were.

Hodur, the blind god, stood by. He didn't join in the circle of gods throwing at Baldur the Beautiful because he was blind.

"Don't you want to join in?" whispered Loki.

"I've got nothing to throw," said Hodur.

"Here," said Loki, and put the mistletoe dart into Hodur's hand. With Loki guiding his arm, Hodur threw the dart. It sped through the air. It hit Baldur, pierced his heart, and the most beautiful of the gods fell dead on the ground.

Silence.

They could not believe that Baldur was dead. But when they realized what had happened, there was a great wailing.

"Who will ride to Helheim, country of the dead," screamed Frigga, "and beg Hela to let Baldur return?"

"I will," said Hermodur. "I will ride the fearful road to Helheim and beg for Baldur's return."

Odin gave him his great horse, Sleipnir, to ride, and he set off on his terrible journey.

Meanwhile, the body of Baldur was carried to the seashore and placed on board his longship. A huge funeral pyre was built on board, and precious jewels and fine clothes decorated the pyre. It was so heavy that only the giantess Hyrrokin could push it out to sea. Thor lighted the pyre, and the burning ship slowly drifted away on the black ocean.

As the ship moved away, a mournful wailing was heard everywhere. When it was at the horizon, the sea and sky seemed to be flaming too. And as it disappeared from view, a ponderous darkness dropped, covered the world like a heavy blanket which muffled all.

Hermodur made his terrible way to Helheim, country of the dead. He rode for nine days and nine nights through the deepest valleys and dales. He passed Gioll, the burning river, and Mogdud, the maiden of Death who guards the bridge to Helheim. He came through the Iron Forest, and when he reached the huge gate of Hela, guarded by the shaggy dog Garm of the Bloody Breast, Sleipnir, Odin's horse, leapt over it.

Hela's hall was cold and damp, and in the grey light Hermodur saw the spirit of Baldur the Beautiful in the seat of honour. Hela herself was half dead and half alive, but Hermodur knelt before her in the gloom.

"I come for Baldur," he pleaded, "that he may return to Asgard."

"Baldur may return," Hela said, "if all that is in the earth weeps for him. But if one thing won't weep, Baldur remains here."

When Hermodur returned with Hela's message, the gods told everything in the world to weep, the beasts, the trees, the stones, even the earth itself, and they all wept for the death of Baldur. But still he did not return.

Hermodur could not believe that Hela would break her word. He knew that something or someone was not weeping, and he set out to find it. At last he came to where sat a giantess. Her eyes were dry as sand.

"Weep for Baldur the Beautiful," said Hermodur.

"Why?" said the giantess.

Hermodur told her.

Then the giantess laughed a harsh, dry laugh like a carrion crow, and said: "I care nothing for your Baldur, beautiful or ugly. Let Hela keep what is hers for ever." And she turned her back and laughed.

So Hermodur rode sadly away, and Baldur stayed in Helheim.

And that was how winter, the Twilight of the Gods, came to Asgard.

But Odin, the most powerful of the gods, knew that one day, long after he and all those who ruled in Asgard were dead, a new sun would shine, a new world would be born, trees would bud, plants shoot up and birds sing again.

St Nicholas

Stained glass window at
Ladbroke Church,
Warwickshire

St Nicholas's Day is 6 December. Nicholas is believed to have been Bishop of Myra in about 320 A.D., but nobody really knows whether this is true.

Many stories are told about St Nicholas. In one, he gives bags of gold to three poor girls for their dowries on their wedding day. (The three bags of gold in the story are the same as the three balls which now hang outside pawnbroker's shops; St Nicholas is the patron saint of pawnbrokers.) In another story, St Nicholas magically heals and brings back to life three little boys who have been chopped up and pickled in a salting-tub to be served up as bacon.

St Nicholas is also the proper name for Santa Claus – Claus being a short form of Ni-*cholas*.

The Boy Bishop

"St Nicholas's Bishop" is a choirboy who is enthroned as Bishop in a sort of mock-pageant on 6 December. From that day until 28 December, Holy Innocents' Day, this boy acts in every way as if he really were the Bishop, and everyone treats him as if he were. At least, that was the original idea when the custom began in Europe over a thousand years ago.

But quite quickly it became something very different from a religious ceremony. The Boy Bishop and the other children led the people in all sorts of merrymaking, acting, dancing, singing and feasting, in the Church.

Because it had become so riotous and disorderly, the ceremony of the Boy Bishop was stopped in England by Henry VIII, and although his daughter Mary tried to restart the custom, it was finally banned by Queen Elizabeth I.

There were many similar customs to that of the Boy Bishop. See what you can find out about the following: the Roman Saturnalia, the Feast of Fools, and the Lord of Misrule. Why do you think that customs like this grew up at this time of the year?

Advent is the period from the fourth Sunday before Christmas until Christmas Day. You could make an Advent calendar, by drawing the calendar on a piece of card, leaving gaps between the days. Then stick a piece of paper over the card, and with a sharp blade cut "windows" over each date. Every morning you open one more window till you reach Christmas.

You could illustrate feast days, such as St Nicholas's Day, with pictures, and you could also use the calendar for recording the weather and your Christmas preparations.

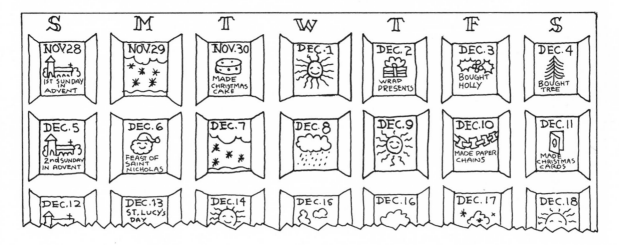

Here is another day for your calendar:

St Thomas grey, St Thomas grey,
Longest night and shortest day.

St Thomas' Day is 21 December. In many parts of the country it was the custom for women to go "a-Thomassing", or "a-gooding". They went round from house to house to collect wheat to make cakes and bread for Christmas. It was also customary for the miller to grind the wheat for them free of charge. In return for the gift of wheat a sprig of holly or mistletoe was given to the householders.

Sometimes the wheat was made into frumenty, which is one of the oldest known English dishes. It was made by soaking the whole grains of wheat in a bowl of water that had to be kept in a warm oven for three days. As a result the grains absorbed the water and swelled and burst. The starch turned the whole mass into a thick jelly which was eaten, like porridge, with sugar and hot milk.

Winter Wise

Walk fast in snow, in frost walk slow,
And still as you go tread on your toe;
When frost and snow are both together,
Sit by the fire, and spare shoe leather.

Traditional

Do you know any other traditional rhymes about the weather? See if you can make a collection of them, especially ones that try to predict the weather, and then keep a record to see if they come true. You could use your Advent calendar to keep your records.

Sheep in Winter

The sheep get up and make their many tracks
And bear a load of snow upon their backs,
And gnaw the frozen turnip to the ground
With sharp quick bite, and then go noising round
The boy who pecks the turnips all the day
And knocks his hands to keep the cold away
And laps his legs in straw to keep them warm
And hides behind the hedges from the storm.
The sheep, as tame as dogs, go where he goes
And try to shake their fleezes from the snows,
Then leave their frozen meal and wander round
The stubble stack that stands beside the ground.

John Clare

Christmas Cards

The first Christmas card was probably invented by Henry Cole, who was also the first director of the Victoria and Albert Museum. The card was designed by John Horsley and 1000 copies of it were made in 1843. It looked like this:

The two pictures on each side represent the charitable acts of "Feeding the Hungry" and "Clothing the Naked", and there is a typical Victorian Christmas scene in the middle. Some later Victorian Christmas cards became very elaborate:

The best Christmas cards are always the ones that you make for people yourself. This could be an individual or class activity and you can use cut-out illustrations from magazines, or all kinds of scraps, as material to stick on card to make them. What kind of things do you usually find on Christmas cards? How can you manage to make some of them from cut-outs and scraps? Use a lot of imagination and you will be surprised at what you can produce. Of course you will also want to include a Christmas and New Year message written as beautifully as possible.

Christmas Carols

At Christmas we hear, on the radio and television, carols which are familiar all over the country. Before the days of mass entertainment, people often had their own local tunes to carols, and sometimes even their own words. Tunes and words like this would be passed on from father to son. Sets of words could also be bought, for they were sold on penny sheets by street pedlars.

While shepherds watched their flocks

While shepherds watched their flocks by night, all seat-ed on the ground,__ The an-gel of the

CHORUS

Lord came down, and glo-ry shone a - round.__ *On that great day, on that great day, on that great day,__*

Christ-ians re-joice_____ with heart and voice,__ Christ is born_ in Beth - le - hem.__

Christ-ians re - joice_____ with heart and voice,__

Christ_ is born_ in Beth - le - hem._____

collected by Roy Palmer, 1971

Antiphonal treatment in chorus.
Drone in verse :

Child carol singers by Phiz (Hablot K. Brown)

This was sung by George Dunn, of Quarry Bank, Staffordshire, who died in 1975 at the age of eighty-seven. How does it differ from the carol you know?
You will probably know the rest of the words. In some verses ("Fear not", "The heavenly babe" and "O glory be"), the chorus changes to "On this great day".
There may be someone in your family, or living near you, who knows local words and tunes for carols. Some of these from the Sheffield area are on the record, "A People's Carol" (Leader Records, LEE 4065).

Make Your Own Christmas Decorations

Paper Chains

Take two very long strips of coloured paper about two inches wide. Place the ends at right angles to each other and glue them together (Fig. 1). Fold the lower strip over the upper (Fig. 2). Continue folding over like this until you've used the whole of each strip (Fig. 3). Loosen the chain. If it is not long enough, other strips may be glued on and the process continued.

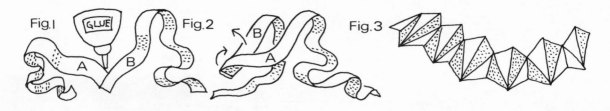

Fig.1   GLUE   A   B   Fig.2   B   A   Fig.3

Decorations with Milk Bottle Tops

Fig.4

Fig.5

Place the top on a flat surface and make eight cuts as shown in Fig. 4, to make eight "petals". Holding the centre in your finger and thumb, twist each petal once (Fig. 5). Pierce the centre with a needle and thread the milk-bottle-top flower on a length of cotton. Plenty of these on the same thread make a chain, and they can be painted.

Make a bell by putting a bottle top over your finger, smoothing it down carefully and then shaping the bottom as in Fig. 6. Knot the end of a piece of cotton and thread it through the top of your bell to hang it up. Again, plenty of these make a chain (Fig. 7). You can make stars, moons and other shapes, and either string them all on a thread, or hang them as a mobile (Fig. 8).

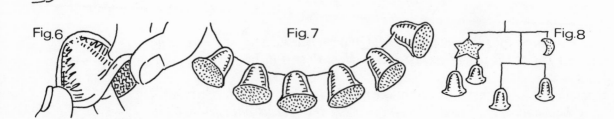

Fig.6   Fig.7   Fig.8

Whirligig

Cut a large circle of stiff card, about 45 cm in diameter, and cut sixteen 5 cm slits at regular intervals round the edge (Fig. 9). Cut a pattern in the card and cover each hole of the pattern with a different-coloured piece of tissue or similar paper. Stick the tissue-paper in place (Fig. 10). Fold one edge of each of the slits downwards to make flaps. Now thread cotton at four opposite points as in Fig. 11, and hang the whirligig from the ceiling. Put a table lamp below it, so that the heat from the lamp turns the whirligig, and the light throws moving patterns of colour through it into the ceiling (Fig. 12).

Fig.9

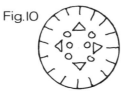
Fig.10

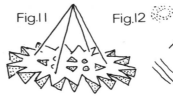
Fig.11

Fig.12

Merry-go-round

Draw a spiral on a piece of stiff card and cut it out (Fig. 13). Thread cotton through the centre and hang it above a fire or radiator. The hot rising air will make it turn. You could hang several on a hoop (Fig. 14), or stick one on a knitting needle which stands in a cork (Fig. 15).

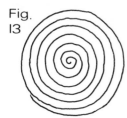
Fig. 13

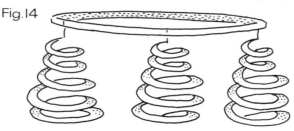
Fig.14

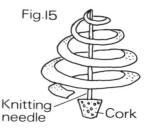
Fig.15

Knitting needle — Cork

Chinese Lantern

Take a rectangle of coloured paper, about 30 cm long and 23 cm wide. Fold it lengthways, and cut strips about 8 cm long upwards from the fold (Fig. 16). Open out the paper, bend it round and glue or sellotape the ends together (Fig. 17). You could stick a strip of paper across the top to act as a handle (Fig. 18). You might like to hang this on the Christmas tree.

Fig.16

Fig.17

Fig.18

Christmas Trees

The Christmas tree was a very old custom in Germany but did not become well established here until the last century. It was especially the one that Prince Albert had at Windsor in 1841 that made the Christmas tree fashionable. Much earlier, the poet, Coleridge, spent Christmas in north Germany in 1798 and he wrote an account of the festivities there:

There is a Christmas custom here which pleased and interested me. The children make little presents to their parents, and to each other, and the parents to their children. . . . On the day before Christmas-day, one of the parlours is lighted up by the children, into which the parents must not go; a great yew bough is fastened on the table at a little distance from the wall, a multitude of little tapers are fixed in the bough, but not so as to burn it till they are nearly consumed, and coloured paper, etc., hangs and flutters from the twigs. Under this bough the children lay out in great order the presents they mean for their parents, still concealing in their pockets what they intend for each other. Then the parents are introduced, and each presents his little gift; they then bring out the remainder one by one, from their pockets, and present them with kisses and embraces. Where I witnessed this scene, there were eight or nine children, and the eldest daughter and the mother wept aloud for joy and tenderness; and the tears ran down the face of the father, and he clasped all his children so tight to his breast, it seemed as if he did it to stifle the sob that was rising within it. I was very much affected. The shadow of the bough and its appendages on the wall, and arching over on the ceiling, made a pretty picture; and then the raptures of the *very* little ones, when at last the twigs and their needles began to take fire and *snap* – O it was a delight to them.

from *The Friend*, 1809

You could draw or paint the scene that Coleridge describes here.

Evergreens

The evergreen was believed to contain magic, because although every-thing else died in winter, evergreens didn't.
See what you can find out about old beliefs concerning:
   holly,
   ivy,
   mistletoe.
(In the story of "The Twilight of the Gods" on pages 2–3, Baldur the Beautiful is killed by a mistletoe dart.)

The Kissing Bough

The Kissing Bough is an old English evergreen decoration that certainly existed long before the Christmas tree became fashionable, and it can still be seen in some homes today. It consists of metal hoops bent into the shape of a crown, which are then covered with evergreens to decorate them and also with apples and lighted candles. A bunch of mistletoe is usually hung underneath, which is how it got its name of kissing bough. It still makes a pretty decoration and you might like to try making one for yourself. It will look something like this:

Usually the Bough was hung just high enough for couples to stand and kiss beneath it. The candles would be lit in the evening on each of the twelve days of Christmas. Round it the carols would be sung in a circle, and under it the Mummers who came to the house with their play would give their performance. It became the centre of the whole festival of Christmas in this way.

You could also make evergreen chains which may have been the origin of the modern paper chain. To do this you need to thread holly leaves and berries alternately on a piece of thread with a needle, keeping the leaf flat by piercing it twice with the needle. It makes a very effective decoration. See what other decorations you can invent using natural things such as evergreen plants as a basis. By doing this you will be taking part in a tradition that goes back for thousands of years.

Try writing about the happiest Christmas that you can remember. What was so special about it?

Mumming Plays

These were plays performed by players who travelled around from house to house at Christmas and New Year, wearing a disguise so that no one could see who they were. The plays were traditional and handed down by word of mouth from one group of players to the next and they were always about the theme of death and rebirth. There was plenty of opportunity for knock-about comedy in the plays. Very similar plays were performed at other times of the year, such as the Pace-Egging Plays at Easter-time. Here is an example of one Mumming Play. You might like to try acting it for yourselves: remember you do not have to stick exactly to the words so long as the general idea of the play is kept. St George was a common Mumming Play hero.

The Play of Good St George and the Bold Hector

Enter (after a loud knock at the door) Open-the-Door.
OPEN-THE-DOOR: The first that doth step in is good old Open-the-
   Door, And lads, if you'll believe me well, I've opened many a score.
*With a sly wink and gesture at this, he proceeds to clear an open space
for the other actors, who have now followed him in, but leave him in the
centre of the stage.*
   Give room, give room in this gallant hall, give us room to play,
   And you shall see a right merry Masque
      Upon this happy Christmas day.
   So shift the chairs, and make a good wide ring,
   That you may see us well, both act and dance and sing.
   Silence, brave gents and lovely ladies fair!
      Now give an eye
   To see and hear our queer quaint comico-Tragedie.
He retires. Saint George takes the centre of the stage.
SAINT GEORGE: Here come I, Saint George, approved of old,
   A Knight of valour and virtue, stout and bold,
   Many the gallant deeds that I have done,
   Clean victories both east and west that I have won.
   In deadly marsh and eke on sandy plain,
   Giants, griffins and rocs in deadly swarms I've slain,
   'Twas I that brought the famed dreaded dragon to slaughter,
   For which I gained the Egyptian Monarch's handsome daughter.
Enter to him Bold Hector.
HECTOR: Who's this that boasts in Hector's hearing?
   Of all braves and braggarts I'll soon make a clearing.
   I am Bold Hector! Bold Hector is my name,
   And with my trusty sword I always win the game!
Enter, smartly, Slasher.

SLASHER: The game, Sir? What game, Sir? This game's not in your
power!
The brave Saint George will slash and slay you dead within the
hour!

Enter, stately, the Black Prince.

PRINCE: Not so fast, my gallant braves and heroes all!
Fair's fair, brave's brave; but when you try a fall,
Sides and chances equal for Englishmen is reckoned –
So see all things square. I'll act for one as second.

SLASHER: Well said, most noble Prince. To make the combat square,
You second good Saint George, and I will see Bold Hector fair.

The two principals and the two seconds prepare their arms.

Enter, deliberately, Safety Sam.

SAM: Hear one last word for peace from Safety Sam of Staffordshire!
Peace is a noble thing though it may be bought too dear,
So ere to mortal strife these noble gallants do repair,
"May God defend the right!" be our one and only prayer.

Enter, with roguish sidling shuffle, Beelzebub.

BEELZEBUB: Here comes I, sly old Beelzebub!
And over my shoulder I carries my club,
And in my hand a frying pan –
So don't you think I'm a jolly old man?
If you think I'm cutting it rather fat,
Just drop a penny in the old man's hat –
A useful penny it is you'll then lay out,
If you want to see the whole of our fine play out.

Enter, impishly and perkily, the little Blue Dwarf.

DWARF: Stand off, stand off! I've fought 10,000 duels on the Delves,
And all you knaves that want to fight had best defend yourselves.
No foe stands up but I'll smash and hash him as small as flies,
And sell his vile carcass to make into nice mince pies,
Mince pies hot, mince pies cold,
Good mince pies at ten days old!

*Black Prince coolly lifts him up bodily, throws him into the arms of
Beelzebub, who carries him out. The two champions, Saint George and
Bold Hector, and their seconds, Black Prince and Slasher, take the
centre and the combat begins. The fencing is done with much dancing
round the ring, loud clashing of swords, and the excited shouts of the
actors. After many fierce lunges and rapid parries and cracks on the head
and legs with the flat of the swords Hector is stabbed and falls prone.*

SLASHER: O champion saint, O holy George! what hast thou done?
Thou hast gone and slain my dear, my only son!
He was indeed my first born and true begotten heir –
I cannot, will not idly stand and see him bleeding there!
A doctor, a doctor, I'll give ten thousand pounds
If but a good and learned doctor can be found!

Enter, slowly and sedately, the Doctor.

DOCTOR: Here comes the great and learned Doctor Brown,
   The cleverest safest doctor in all the town,
   Crutches for lame ducks make I, spectacles for poor blind bats,
   Also barber-leech I am, to shave and bleed all pussy cats.
   I've travelled far in Italy, Titaly, Dudley Port and Old Spain,
   But right glad I am to be once more in Old Wednesbury again.

SLASHER: What diseases, sir, are they you cure?

DOCTOR: Why, all diseases known, you may be sure;
   The gout, the scurvy and the ptysic.
   So –

taking Hector gravely and skilfully by the hand
      you get up, sir, and sing that fine old song
   Of one who's not been dead for very long.

Hector rises erect again.

HECTOR: Once I was dead but now I am alive,
   God bless the Doctor, who made me to survive!
   Through his great art I was not dead for very long
   And so to prove his skill, let me sing you a live man's song!

He sings some popular song of the day, which has a chorus in which all can join.

BEELZEBUB: Our play is played and now we've done,
   We hope we've given you lots of simple fun,
   So if you think at all it's really funny,
   You'll fill our empty pokes with lots of money.
   Send us away, please, now that all is calm,
   And sly old Beelzebub'll do you no harm.
   Take notice that we've got no leathern bottle,
   And nothing was poured down the dead man's throttle.
   For your fun 'twas he fought, and got himself slain,
   For your money he'll rise and fight his battles o'er again.
   We hope your spirits this nonsense will joyful rouse,
   So we bid you Good-day and Peace be on this noble house!

All join hands to dance round, to the accompaniment of some other popular song – which at the end is changed to one which they march out to, Beelzebub collecting the largesse in his frying pan.

from *Staffordshire Customs, Superstitions and Folklore*, 1924,
by F. W. Hackwood

This version of a Mumming Play comes from Staffordshire and uses local place names. You could easily adapt it to fit your own particular locality.

Troll Feast

Per Gynt was a hunter. He was proud and strong, and he laughed at fear.

One day, late in the year, towards Christmas, he decided to go into the mountains. In Norway, in the winter, all the cattle are brought down from the hills and the mountains, and men say the Trolls run free over the fells. But Per didn't care. He went into the mountains.

He knew of a shepherd's hut where he thought he could spend the night. But by the time he reached the hut, it was so dark that he couldn't even see his own hand when he held it in front of his eyes. It was dark as blindness.

His foot struck something. It moved. Per Gynt put his hand down and grabbed hold of something cold and slimy.

"What are you?" he asked.

"I am the Crooked One," it croaked.

"Well, crooked or straight, you'd better get out of my way," said Per Gynt. It seemed to shift, and Per Gynt went on into the hut.

Just inside the hut, his foot struck something. It was cold and slimy, and it moved.

"What are you now?" said Per.

"I am the Crooked One," it croaked.

Per Gynt moved again, but each time he moved he bumped into the cold, slimy thing, and each time its croaky voice told him it was the Crooked One. Finally Per stood still.

"Get out of my hut," he shouted. "Or I'll shoot."

The Crooked One just laughed. Per Gynt aimed his gun and shot it three times through the head. The hollow, croaky laugh went on. Per stopped shooting.

"Shoot again," croaked the voice.

But Per knew better. If he had shot a fourth time, the bullet would have bounced back and killed him. So Per and his dogs just took hold of the great slimy thing and dragged it out of the hut. And the hills echoed with mocking laughter.

Then Per went back into the hut and lit a fire to boil his kettle of soup. But the fire began to smoke, so he had to knock a hole in the wall to let the smoke out. No sooner had he done so than a great big nose was stuck into the room through the hole.

"How do you like my smeller?" said a Troll's voice.

"How do you like my soup?" said Per Gynt, and poured the boiling soup over the nose.

The Troll rushed away, shrieking in pain, and the hills echoed with mocking laughter, and cries of: "Soup smeller! Soup smeller!"

Then everything went quiet. Per waited. Soon he could hear noises coming closer, whispering voices and silly laughter. Per looked

through the hole he'd made in the wall, and saw them – Troll gangs. He waited.

Suddenly a bucketful of water came down the chimney. The fire hissed and went out. Per was left in the dark again. Mocking laughter and taunts came from all over the place. "Now, Per Gynt, now what are you going to do?"

Per Gynt swore revenge.

He went home. But on Christmas Eve he set out once again for the mountains, to a farm he knew which the Trolls used for their feasting. He took with him a tame bear and some tools of the shoemaker's trade. When he reached the farm he knocked on the door and asked for shelter.

"Shelter!" said the farmer. "We can't help you. We can't even help ourselves – we're just leaving. The Trolls will be coming soon."

But Per wasn't worried. So while the farmer and his wife left their home, Per Gynt stayed. The bear lay down under the settle by the hearth, and Per took a pig's skin and made it into a huge shoe, using a rope for the shoelace.

Suddenly the Trolls arrived, with fiddles and fiddlers, and began to dance their Christmas revels. Christmas food was brought in to make a mighty feast, with laughing and scoffing. They ate fried frogs and toads and things like that, and washed it down with black wine. Some of them noticed the shoe Per Gynt had made, the enormous pig-skin shoe. They started laughing. One Troll put his foot in it. Then another did. Then it was a game: how many Trolls could get a foot in the shoe?

Just when the whole lot of them had squeezed a foot into it, Per Gynt leapt out of his hiding place and pulled the rope lace tight. He tied it, and every Troll was trapped.

"Now, Bruin!" shouted Per to the bear. "Would you like your Christmas dinner?"

The bear shambled out.

"Would you like a piece of cake, pussy?" shouted one of the Trolls, and threw a scalding fried frog in the bear's face.

The bear was furious. He rushed among the captured Trolls, swiping and scratching them horribly, and Per picked up a spare stick and laid into them, too. The Trolls pulled and struggled, and got in each other's way, in their efforts to escape. At last they broke free, and ran and stumbled and staggered to the door, and streamed away across the hillside.

Per Gynt laughed loudly at their confusion. Then he set about making his own Christmas dinner, and he ate it all alone with no further ado.

As for the Trolls, no one heard a whisper from them for many a long year.

This story would make an excellent mime or dance drama.

The Norwegian composer, Edward Grieg, wrote The Peer Gynt Suite *for a play about Per Gynt by Henrik Ibsen, and you could probably use parts of it to accompany your mime or dance. But you will probably want more music and sound effects than this. You might try using electronic music, or, better still, you might try and make some suitable music of your own.*

Make hideous masks for the trolls, and a suitable costume for the bear.

If you can use lighting effects for different scenes, that could be very effective.

Split the story into scenes and rehearse one scene at a time before putting it all together. It should be an exciting piece to perform at an assembly or in the lunch hour for the rest of the school.

Blow, Blow, Thou Winter Wind

Blow, blow, thou winter wind,
Thou art not so unkind
   As man's ingratitude;
Thy tooth is not so keen,
Because thou art not seen,
   Although thy breath be rude.
Heigh-ho! sing, heigh-ho! unto the green holly:
Most friendship is feigning, most loving mere folly.
   Then heigh-ho! the holly!
    This life is most jolly.

Freeze, freeze, thou bitter sky,
That does not bite so nigh
   As benefits forgot:
Though thou the waters warp,
Thy sting is not so sharp
   As friend remembered not.
Heigh-ho! sing, heigh-ho! unto the green holly:
Most friendship is feigning, most loving mere folly.
   Then heigh-ho! the holly!
    This life is most jolly.

from *As You Like It* by William Shakespeare

Christmas Dinner

Mrs Cratchit made the gravy (ready beforehand in a little saucepan) hissing hot: Master Peter mashed the potatoes with incredible vigour; Miss Belinda sweetened up the apple sauce; Martha dusted the hot plates . . . At last, Mrs Cratchit, looking slowly all along the carving-knife, prepared to plunge it into the breast; but when she did, and when the long-expected gush of stuffing issued forth, one murmur of delight arose all round the board. . . .

There never was such a goose. Bob said he didn't believe there ever was such a goose cooked. Its tenderness and flavour, size and cheapness, were the themes of universal admiration. Eked out by apple sauce and mashed potatoes, it was a sufficient dinner for the whole family; indeed, as Mrs Cratchit said with great delight (surveying one small atom of a bone upon the dish), they hadn't ate it all at last! Yet every one had had enough, and the youngest Cratchits, in particular, were steeped in sage and onion to the eyebrows! But now, the plates being changed by Miss Belinda, Mrs Cratchit left the room alone – too nervous to bear witnesses – to take the pudding up, and bring it in.

A great deal of steam! The pudding was out of the copper. A smell like a washing-day! That was the cloth. A smell like an eating-house and a pastry cook's next door to each other, with a laundress's next door to that! That was the pudding! In half a minute Mrs Cratchit entered – flushed but smiling proudly – with the pudding, like a speckled cannon-ball, so hard and firm, blazing in half a half-a-quartern of ignited brandy, and bedight with Christmas holly stuck into the top.

Oh, a wonderful pudding! Bob Cratchit said, and calmly too, that he regarded it as the greatest success achieved by Mrs Cratchit since their marriage . . . they were happy, grateful, pleased with one another, and contented with the time. . . .

from *A Christmas Carol* by Charles Dickens

This would be a good scene to act. Try doing so, making up the conversation around the table from the hints given in the description.

Christmas Dinner, 1836, by Robert Seymour

The Boar's Head

The tradition of eating a Boar's Head on Christmas Day has been kept up at the Queen's College in Oxford since 1340. The bringing in of the Boar's Head is accompanied by the singing of "The Boar's Head Carol", which was first printed in 1521.

Bringing in the Boar's head at Queen's College, Oxford, 1846, by J. L. Williams

The Boar's Head Carol

The boar's head in hand bear I, Be-decked with bays and rose-ma-ry; I pray you, my mas-ters,

be mer-ry, *Quot est-is in con-vi-vi-o.* *Cap-ut ap-ri de-fer-o,* *Red-dens lau-des Do-mi-no.*

The boar's head, as I understand,	Our steward hath provided this
Is the fairest dish in all the land,	In honour of the King of Bliss;
When thus bedecked with a gay garland,	Which on this day to be servèd is
Let us *servire cantico.*	*In regimensi atrio.*

Repeat first verse.

from *Popular Music of the Olden Time*, 1859, W. Chappell

Add the ceremonial touch of a big drum in minims. Second part for the last three bars.

The Latin words mean: "As many as are at the feast" (verse 1), "I carry in the boar's head, while giving praise to the Lord" (chorus), "serve while singing" (verse 2), and "in the squire's hall' (verse 3).

Father Christmas

When I was younger I thought Father Christmas was a wonderful man. On Christmas Eve before I went to bed I would make my mother put out the fire. I was afraid that Father Christmas would get burnt when he climbed down the chimney. My sister would write out my Christmas list (because I couldn't write) and I would throw it up the chimney. When I went to town with my mother, I wondered how Father Christmas could be in all the stores at once. She told me they were his brothers and the real one came on Christmas Eve. My sister would make a cup of tea and biscuits for him. But when I got to the age of six the older children called me silly because I believed in Father Christmas. When I got home I asked my mother and she said, "Of course there's a Father Christmas," but I did not believe her.

from *The Lore and Language of Schoolchildren* by I. and P. Opie

People often leave something out for Father Christmas when he calls, sometimes a piece of cake and a glass of sherry.

What customs were there in your household when you were younger which you carried out on Christmas Eve; if you have younger brothers and sisters you may still carry them out at home?

At what age did you stop believing in Father Christmas? You could conduct a class survey to see if it happened to each of you at about the same age.

Sometimes children go on pretending to believe in Father Christmas after they have really ceased to do so. Why might this be? – to please their parents, because they think they will get more presents that way, or to try to hang on to a piece of their childhood, perhaps? How did you feel about it when you found out the truth?

Carol

There was a Boy bedded in bracken,
Like to a sleeping snake all curled he lay;
On his thin navel turned this spinning sphere,
Each feeble finger fetched seven suns away.
He was not dropped in good-for-lambing weather,
He took no suck when shook buds sing together,
But he is come in cold-as-workhouse weather,
Poor as a Salford child.

John Short

Plum Puddings

Plum puddings for Christmas need to be made well in advance. The traditional date is known as "Stir Up Sunday". It is the Sunday before Advent and the Collect in the service for that day is as follows:

Stir up we beseech thee, O Lord, the wills of thy faithful people, that they plenteously bringing forth the fruit of good works may of thee be plenteously rewarded.

The first two words of the Collect led to this name for the day itself and it seemed a good day on which to prepare the puddings. Everyone in the family is supposed to have a stir and to make a wish for good luck. It is customary to put a silver coin in the pudding for good luck. It used to be a silver farthing but now it would have to be five pence. A silver thimble and a ring were often put in too. The thimble was supposed to mean a happy life for the one who got it; the ring meant a marriage would happen in the coming year.

We would not very much like the puddings in this song however:

Black, White, Yellow and Green

She took and put them in the pot,
She boiled them till they were blazing hot.

Oh, she took a pin and pricked the skin;
The gravy ran out and the maggots ran in.

Oh, she took and put them on the floor;
They each in turn ran out of the door.

Oh, she took and put them on the shelf;
If you want any more you must help yourself.

traditional

23

Boxing Day

The day after Christmas Day, 26 December, is called Boxing Day because it was the day when servants and tradesmen were given their Christmas gifts, or Christmas "boxes". Here is how William Tayler, a footman, describes Boxing Day in London in 1837:

This is what is called about here Boxing Day. It's the day the people goe from house to house gathering their Christmas boxes. We have had numbers here today – sweeps, beadles, lamplighters, waterman, dustmen, scavengers (that is the men who clean the mud out of the streets), newspaper boy, general postmen, twopenny postmen* and waits. These are a set of men that goe about the streets playing musick in the night after people are in bed and a sleepe. Some people are very fond of hearing them, but for my own part, I don't admire being roused from a sound sleep by a whole band of musick and perhaps not get to sleep again for an houre or two. All these people expect to have a shilling or half a crown each. Went out this morning, saw plenty of people rowling about the streets in the hight of their glorey . . . Miss P. gave me half a sovering for a Christmas box, one of the trades people gave me half a crown, another gave me a shilling. I mite get fuddled two or three times a day if I had a mind, as all the trades people that serve this house are very pressing with their glass of something to drink their health this Christmas time . . .

* The Twopenny Post, serving the London area, was distinct from the General Post. The two services overlapped badly and were combined in 1854.

from *Diary of William Tayler, Footman, 1837*, ed. by Dorothy Wise

26 December is also the day of the first Christian martyr, St Stephen. See what you can find out about St Stephen.

The following song was often sung on Boxing Day by parties of children going round from door to door, and hoping that their story would touch the hearts and open the pockets of householders. At Ripon, in Yorkshire, the hero was a sailor boy, and in other parts of the country, a smuggler's boy.

The Soldier's Boy

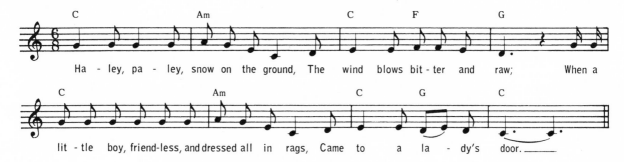

Ha - ley, pa - ley, snow on the ground, The wind blows bit - ter and raw; When a lit - tle boy, friend-less, and dressed all in rags, Came to a la - dy's door.

As the lady sat at her window so high,
He raised both his eyes with joy:
"Oh lady gay, take pity I pray,
On a poor little soldier's boy.

"My mother died when I was young,
And father went to the wars;
In battle brave he nobly fell,
All covered with wounds and scars.

"But many miles on his knapsack
He carried me with joy,
But now I'm left, of pity bereft,
A poor little soldier's boy.

"As through the streets I wander and roam,
I often heave a sigh;
When children run to their parents' home,
No home nor friends have I.

"At times when hunger gnaws my heart
I sit me down and cry;
Then pity take, for mercy's sake,
On a poor little soldier's boy".

Then the lady rushed from her window so high,
And opened her mansion door:
"Come in, come in, unfortunate lad,
You never shall wander more.

"For my only son in battle fell,
He was my only joy;
And while I live I'll shelter give
To a poor little soldier's boy".

text adapted from Pitts broadside
tune collected by Mr David Hillery from his mother, Mrs Lilian Hillery of Ripon

25

Pantomime

In every big city, and in plenty of smaller towns, the theatres at Christmas put on pantomimes. Although the earliest pantomimes in the eighteenth century had nothing to do with Christmas they have now been part of the Christmas festivities for a hundred years or more, and they are no longer produced at other times of the year. Here is a description of a boy's visit to the famous Drury Lane pantomime, nearly a hundred years ago:

A sharp tap on his desk by the conductor of the orchestra calls everyone to order. In a second there is a hush, a silence. And then – oh glorious moment in the Christmas life of a town-bred child – the overture to the pantomime commences! What overture can ever equal a first-rate overture to a pantomime on the first night of performance? What drawings-in of breath, all of a quiver! Fine parts for the deep bass of the brass, splendid chances for bassoon, cymbals and drums of all sorts and sizes! Crash! bang! – the green curtain has long ago disappeared, showing the gay "act-drop" behind it. And now after the final fortissimo, followed by deafening applause, the facing round of the conductor in order to bow his acknowledgments to the audience and, it may be, to finish up with "God save the Queen" and *then* a great silence, the orchestra plays mysterious music and – oh joy, yet dread and terror! – the curtain rises on some gloomy cave of fearful demons whose nearer acquaintance not a boy among us under eight years of age would be eager to cultivate.

Afterwards came the good fairies, the sprites, and before ten o'clock we were roaring with laughter at Joey the Clown and were joining the audience in the uproarious demand for "Hot Codlins", which song sent us all into convulsions of laughter, especially when the Clown imitated the little old woman (the heroine of the song) who, as was related, was deposited "on her latter – head?" asked the simple Clown. "No – end," shouted the audience, knowingly but rudely. Whereupon the Clown winked and, rejecting the suggestion, went at once into the highly intelligent chorus, which was, I fancy, "Rum-ti-tiddy-iddytiddy-iddy", with which everyone was so enraptured that nothing but its treble encore would satisfy them.

The whacking, the banging, the horse-play, the tomfoolery of the "comic scenes" of those ancient pantomimes! Well, it certainly did delight the children: we gloried in the Harlequin, loved the Columbine to desperation, loved the Clown and were ready to bully and laugh at the poor old doting Pantaloon. . . . Everything was over, blue and red fire and all, by eleven, and we children went home to bed, so very happy, but oh, so very tired.

Sir F. C. Burnand

A Project on Pantomime

Find out something of the history of the pantomime. Pantomime: A
Story in Pictures *by Raymond Mander and Joe Mitchenson is the best
book for this, but there will probably be others in your library.*

What is a Harlequinade?

*Find out something about the life of one of the great pantomime clowns,
e.g. John Rich, Joey Grimaldi or Dan Leno.*

*If you've been to a pantomime, you've probably noticed how little
"story" there is, and how much of other things — singing, dancing,
comedy, conjuring, stage "effects", audience joining in, and so on. Why
do you think this is? Try and describe some of these "extra" bits as
accurately as you can.*

Would you like to see a pantomime on ice? Why?

*What do you think is gained by the old practice of a girl playing the
main boy's part, and a man playing the "dame"?*

*Find out about some famous pantomime characters, e.g. Abanazar,
Widow Twankey, Buttons, the Ugly Sisters, Tinkerbell, etc. Write
about their parts in the stories. Act a scene in which the character you've
chosen appears.*

*Find out about children working in pantomime and in other branches
of entertainment. Why do you think actors often say they will never act
with "children or animals"? Why do you think so many T.V. advertise-
ments use children?*

Joey Grimaldi as Clown, Tom Ellar as Harlequin and James Barnes as Pantaloon
in an early nineteenth-century pantomime

Hunting the Wren

A wren-house from Marloes, Pembrokeshire (approx. 30 cm long)

A rather cruel Boxing Day custom was the Hunting of the Wren, which also sometimes took place on Twelfth Night. The custom is very old and it may have something to do with the name of "the Devil's bird" that the wren is given in some parts of England and Ireland. The reason for the association with Boxing Day may be an old tradition that it was the singing of the wren that gave away St Stephen, whose martyrdom is remembered on 26 December. An Irish rhyme refers to the wren hunt:

> The wren, the king of all the birds,
> Was caught on St Stephen's day in the furze.

In some places, such as Pembrokeshire, the wren was paraded round the village in a little house when it had been caught. Here it was thought that the procession and singing would bring good luck in the coming year. This is the kind of song that would be sung:

28

Hunting the Wren

'Oh where are you go-ing?' says Mil-der to Mel-der; 'Oh, where are you go-ing?' says the young-er to the el-der. 'Oh, I can-not tell,' says Fes-tel to Fose. 'We're go-ing to the woods,'— said John the Red Nose; 'We're go-ing to the woods,' said John the Red Nose

"Oh, what will you do there?" *etc.*
"Oh, what will you do there?" *etc.*
"Oh, I cannot tell," *etc.*
"We'll shoot the Cutty Wren," *etc.*
"We'll shoot the Cutty Wren," *etc.*

"Oh, how will you shoot her?"
"Oh, how will you shoot her?"
"Oh, I cannot tell"
"With arrows and bows"

"Oh, that will not do"
"Oh, that will not do"
"Oh, what will do then?"
"Big cannons and guns"

"Oh, how will you bring her home?"
"Oh, how will you bring her home?"
"Oh, I cannot tell"
"On four strong men's shoulders"

"Oh, that will not do"
"Oh, that will not do"
"Oh, what will do then?"
"In waggons and carts"

"Oh, how will you cut her up?"
"Oh, how will you cut her up?"
"Oh, I cannot tell"
"With knives and with forks"

"Oh, that will not do"
"Oh, that will not do"
"Oh, what will do then?"
"With hatchets and cleavers"

"Oh, how will you boil her?"
"Oh, how will you boil her?"
"Oh, I cannot tell"
"In kettles and pots"

"Oh, that will not do"
"Oh, that will not do"
"Oh, what will do then?"
"In cauldrons and pans"

"Oh, who'll have the spare ribs?"
"Oh, who'll have the spare ribs?"
"Oh, I cannot tell"
"We'll give 'em to the poor"

traditional; tune from *Welsh Goblins*, 1880, by W. Sikes

Ostinato as shown, played on glockenspiel, or sung. Indian bell or triangle played once at the beginning of each bar may add to excitement.

New Year

Ring out, wild bells, to the wild sky,
   The flying cloud, the frosty light:
   The year is dying in the night;
Ring out, wild bells, and let him die.

Ring out the old, ring in the new,
   Ring, happy bells, across the snow:
   The year is going, let him go;
Ring out the false, ring in the true.

from In Memoriam *by Alfred Lord Tennyson*

Dydd Calan yw hi heddiw,
Rwy'n dyfod ar eich traws
I mofyn am y geiniog
Neu grwst o fara caws.
O dewch i'r drws yn siriol
Heb newid dim o'ch gwedd;
Cyn daw dydd Calan eto
Bydd llawer yn y bedd.

(It's New Year's Day and I'm coming to ask you for a penny or bread and cheese. Come to the door smiling. Before next New Year's Day many will be in their graves.)

from The Lore and Language of Schoolchildren *by I. and P. Opie*

New Year Customs

There are lots of customs associated with the new year: we sing "Auld Lang Syne", kiss each other, usually have something to drink and a piece of cake, and go "first-footing". In this custom the idea is that the first person to enter the house in the New Year should be dark-haired and this is thought to bring good luck to the household for the coming year. Ideally he ought to bring with him a piece of wood or coal to put on the fire as this will mean that the house will never be without warmth during the year either. There are many variations on this custom and many different ways of celebrating the new year in different parts of the country.

What do you do at New Year? Have you any special ways of celebrating in your household? Tell each other about them and perhaps, make up a class booklet of New Year customs. You could include any special games that you play at this time of the year as well.

Lucky Bird, Lucky Bird

Lucky bird, lucky bird, chuck, chuck, chuck!
Master and mistress, it's time to get up.
If you don't get up, you'll have no luck,
Lucky bird, lucky bird, chuck, chuck, chuck!

from *Yorkshire Dialect Poems*, 1916, by F. W. Moorman

Yorkshire children used to go round chanting this rhyme on New Year's morning. The "lucky bird" was the dark-haired boy who could let in the New Year and bring good luck.

A Riddle

Q: When do Christmas Day and New Year's Day fall in the same year?

A: Every year – but not in that order.

Coventry God-cakes

Made on New Year's Day when children visit their godparents.

Use puff pastry. Mix 100 g currants, 25 g peel, all spice and nutmeg, 50 g sugar and 25 g butter in a pan and heat for a few minutes. Then cool in a basin. Roll out your pastry and cut into triangles. Put a good tablespoon of mixture in each triangle. Rolling-pin them and make a hole in the top of the crust. Then 10–15 minutes in a hot oven. Sprinkle with castor sugar according to the sweetness of your godchild.

New Year Recipe from Scotland

Bonnach-Nollaig (New Year Bannock)
Oatmeal, butter and caraway seed. Put sufficient quantity of meal in a basin and rub the butter well through it. Put in the caraway seed, mix up the whole. Add water until the dough is a proper consistency, turn out, and knead the bannock about an inch thick. Place a cup with its mouth downwards on the centre of the bannock, cut round the cup with a sharp knife. Cut round the outer edges of the bannock with the knife, pinch the edges with the finger and thumb, put the bannock on a griddle or brander, and bake over a clear fire.

The Mari Lwyd
(Welsh New Year Custom)

The Mari Lwyd procession at a cottage door
in Llangynwyd, Glamorgan, *c.* 1909

No one quite knows what Mari Lwyd means – perhaps Grey Mare, or Holy Mary. The name was given to the figure of a horse which was carried from door to door in parts of Wales during the twelve days of Christmas. The party with the horse first sang a song asking permission to go into the house, and also issuing a challenge to a competition in making up verses. A little later, someone from the house would take up the challenge, and he and one of the Mari Lwyd party would exchange verses, to the same music, in which they made fun of each other's habits – drunkenness, miserliness, for example, or even singing. These verses were partly made up on the spot, and partly traditional. No doubt the Mari Lwyd singers had more practice than those they visited, for the debate usually ended with their winning, and being invited in. After sampling the cake and ale, and perhaps being given money, they would leave, but not before giving a farewell song.

A Most Extraordinary Apparition

At eight o'clock I was sitting with some other people round the fire, when we heard tramping outside, and a loud knocking on the door, which was locked. There was the sound of a flute a moment later, and a man began singing – I could not distinguish the words – then a few minutes later another man, inside the room, went to the door and sang what was apparently an answer to the song without. Then the door was thrown open, and in walked about a dozen people, headed by a most extraordinary apparition, an animal covered with a flowing sheet, and surmounted by a horse's skull, to which a bridle was attached. This apparition I saw a moment later, was really a man covered with a sheet; his head was bowed down, and a skull had been fastened on to it. The people sang, collected some money, and then went off; they ought by rights, apparently, to have had an ass's skull, but then, dead donkeys are proverbially hard to come by.

from a manuscript by Francis Kilvert

You could try making up a rhyming contest along the lines of the Mari Lwyd for yourselves, perhaps between the two halves of the class.

Cân y Fari Lwyd (The Mari Lwyd Song)

Wel, dym - a ni'n dyw - ad, Gyf - eill - ion di - niw - ad, I of - yn (o)s ciawn
Well, here we are com - ing, The best of com - pan - ions, To ask your per -

gan - nad, I of - yn (o)s ciawn gan-nad, I of - yn (o)s ciawn gan - nad I___ gian - u.
mis - sion, To ask your per - mis - sion. To ask your per - mis - sion To___ sing.

Os na chawn ni gannad,	Now if we don't have leave,
Rhowch glywad ar ganiad	Oh listen to our song,
Pa fodd ma'r'madawiad (3)	Whatever the parting (3)
Nos heno.	This night.
Ni dorson ein crimpa	We did not break our legs
Wrth groeshi'r sticila	When crossing the stiles
I ddyfod tuag yma (3)	When we were a-coming (3)
Nos heno.	This night.
Os oes yna ddynion	If there are some men here
All dorri anglynion,	Who can write some verses,
Rhowch glywad yn union (3)	Please give your attention (3)
Nos heno.	This night.
Os aethoch rhy gynnar	If you went too early,
I'r gwely'n ddialgar,	Disgruntled, to your bed,
O, codwch yn hawddgar (3)	Now get up sweet-tempered (3)
Nos heno.	This feast.
Y dishan fras felys	The rich cake is so sweet,
Â phob sort o sbeisys,	With all sorts of spices,
O, torrwch hi'n rhatus (3)	So cut a good helping (3)
Y Gwyla.	This feast.
O, tapwch y baril	And tap the big barrel,
A 'llengwch a'n rhugul;	And let it flow freely,
Na rannwch a'n gynnil (3)	And pour a good glassful (3)
Y Gwyla.	This feast.

from *Caneuon Llafar Gwlad*, Vol. 1, 1975, ed. by D. Roy Saer
translated by O. Griffiths and Roy Palmer

The Rightwise King of All England

The realm of England stood in danger. When no king reigns in the land, every lord thinks himself a petty king. So it was in England after the death of Uther Pendragon.

Merlin went to the Archbishop of Canterbury and advised him to send for all the lords of the realm to come to London at Christmas, for Merlin knew of a miracle which would happen then to show who should be King.

So all the lords of the realm came. On Christmas Day, when they were in church, there was seen in the churchyard a great block of stone, and raised in the middle of it, a thing like an anvil made of steel. A sword was stuck in the anvil so that only the hilt showed, and round it was written in letters of gold:
WHOSO PULLETH OUT THIS SWORD OF THIS STONE AND ANVIL IS RIGHTWISE KING BORN OF ALL ENG-LAND.

When they saw this, many of the lords tried to pull out the sword, hoping to prove themselves King. But none could budge it an inch.

"He's not here," said the Archbishop of Canterbury, "whoever is going to pull out the sword. But he will be made known to us."

So the matter rested for a whole week, until New Year's Day, when all the lords and knights gathered again for a jousting tournament.

Sir Ector, who had rich lands near London, rode to the joust, and with him Sir Kay, his son, and young Arthur, who had been brought up by Sir Ector as though he was Kay's brother. As they rode towards the field, Sir Kay discovered he had no sword, he had left it at his father's house, and now he begged Arthur to go back and fetch it for him.

Arthur agreed and rode away.

But when he got to Sir Ector's house, the doors were all fast shut – everyone had gone to watch the sport. Arthur was very annoyed. He said to himself: "I'll ride to the churchyard and take the sword that's stuck into the stone there. My brother Kay is not going without a sword today." So he rode to the churchyard, and there he dismounted and tied his horse to the stile. He walked over to the stone block, carelessly grasped the sword's handle in his hand, and lightly and fiercely pulled it out of the stone. And then he took his horse again and rode till he came to Sir Kay. He put the sword in Sir Kay's hands.

As soon as Sir Kay saw it, he knew the sword. He found his father, Sir Ector, and said: "Look – the sword from the stone. I must be King of all England."

Sir Ector looked at the sword, recognized it.

"Come back to the churchyard with me," he said, and Kay and young Arthur followed him.

At the church, standing on holy ground, Sir Ector made Sir Kay put his hand on the book and swear how the sword came to him.

"My brother Arthur brought it to me," said Sir Kay.

"How did you get it?" Sir Ector said to Arthur.

Arthur explained how he'd gone back for Sir Kay's sword, but there was nobody at home to let him in; and how, thinking Kay should still have a sword, he had come here and pulled it out of the stone without any difficulty.

Sir Ector looked at Arthur. Then he said: "Now I understand. You are King of all England."

"Why?" said Arthur.

"Why?" said Sir Ector. "Because God will have it so. Nobody can pull this sword from this stone except the rightwise king of all England. Let me see whether you can put the sword back as it was and pull it out again."

"There's no trickery in it," said Arthur, and he put the sword back in the stone.

Then Sir Ector tried to pull it out. But he couldn't. And Sir Kay pulled at it with all his might, but it never moved an inch.

"Now you try again," said Sir Ector to Arthur.

And Arthur drew it out easily.

Sir Ector kneeled down on the earth in front of him, and so did Sir Kay.

"My father – and my brother – why do you kneel to me?"

"No, my lord Arthur, no, it is not so. I was never your father, nor any blood relation of yours. And I think now you are of higher blood than I ever imagined." And Sir Ector told Arthur how Merlin had brought him to him as a little baby, to look after and feed and teach. And now Sir Ector understood Merlin's actions.

Then Arthur's heart hurt that Sir Ector, whom he loved, was not his father.

"And will you be my good and gracious lord when you are King?" asked Sir Ector.

"If not, I were to blame," said Arthur. "You are the man in the world I owe most to, and my good lady, my mother, your wife, who cared for me and kept me as if I was one of her own . . ."

They went to the Archbishop of Canterbury and told him how the sword was drawn out, and by whom. And after he had demonstrated to the doubting lords how he drew the sword, which they could not, Arthur became King of all England.

And all this happened on the first day of the New Year.

adapted from The Tale of King Arthur by Thomas Malory

King Arthur

King Arthur is one of Britain's most famous heroes. His story, sometimes known as "The Matter of Britain", can be researched and recreated in story, poem and play in as many ways as you can think of. A good start would be to read The Sword at Sunset *by R. Sutcliff, then to take an incident and make your own ballad of it.*

Alternatively, you could begin by doing some research. Find out where Arthur's Seat, or other places named after Arthur, are, and mark them on a map of Britain. Are there any to visit in your area? Glastonbury and Cadbury Castle in Somerset are perhaps the best known places associated with Arthur. Try to find out as much of the truth (rather than the legends) about Arthur as you can. Two good books to start such a search from are: The Quest for Arthur's Britain, *edited by Geoffrey Ashe (Paladin Books), and* King Arthur in Legend and History *by Richard Barber (Cardinal Books). A rather simpler book is* The Search for King Arthur *by C. Hibbert (A Cassell Caravel Book).*

Galahad comes to take his place in the Perilous Seat,
from a fourteenth century manuscript

Twelfth Night

Firing at the apple-tree, in Devonshire

6 January, Twelfth Night, is the official end of the Twelve Days of Christmas. It marks the end of the festivities and it is the night on which Christmas decorations are usually taken down. To leave them, or the Christmas cards, on display after this is thought to bring bad luck to the household.

In the south-west, where there are many apple trees, a custom survives known as "wassailing the apple trees", which is intended to ensure that the trees bear well in the coming apple harvest.

The custom of wassailing was one that lasted from Christmas until Twelfth Night. The word was originally *wes heill*, meaning "be whole". *Heill* still exists in our language in the expression "hale and hearty". Do you know what this means? "Wassail", then, was used to wish people good health when they were drinking. Do you know any other expressions of this kind?

On Twelfth Night groups of people, rather like carol singers, used to go round visiting the houses and farms to wish them good health for the coming year by singing a wassail song. The householders and farmers would give them money or food and spiced ale, and the wassailers carried a special bowl for the ale.

As well as singing the wassail song to wish the apple trees good health it was often the custom that the wassailers would fire guns, and stamp and shout, to frighten away the evil spirits that might bring bad luck. Often a piece of cake was left in the branches as a present.

Apple Tree Wassail

Old ap-ple tree we'll wass-ail thee, And hop-ing thou wilt bear.__ The Lord does know where

we shall be To be mer-ry an-oth-er year.__ To_ blow well and to bear well And so

mer-ry let us be;__ Let ev-'ry man drink up his cup, And_ health to the old ap-ple tree.__

(Spoken):
Apples now, hatfuls, capfuls, three-bushel bagfuls, tallets
'olefuls, barn's floorfuls, little heap under the stairs.
(Shouted):
Hip, hip, hip, hooray.
(Stamp, cheer, fire off guns).

from *Cecil Sharp's Collection of English Folk Songs*, Vol. 2, ed. by M. Karpeles

"To blow" here means to blossom, and "tallets" are hay lofts.

Hên phiol fuddiol, lawn foddion, – llyniwd
Er llonmi cyfeillion.
Hoff anwyl, dyma'r ffynnon,
Difyr o hyd yw dwfr hon.

Old beneficial bowl, full of medicine,
Designed to make friends merry.
Dearest beloved, this is the well,
Pleasant is the water it contains.

The Welsh rhyme is on a seventeenth century wassail bowl in the Ceredigion Museum at Aberystwyth (above). Other bowls can be found in museums and houses up and down the country.

Wassail Bowl

3 l brown ale; ½ kg soft brown sugar; 1 large stick of cinnamon; 1 level teaspoon grated nutmeg; ½ level teaspoon ground ginger; 2 lemons thinly sliced; 1 bottle medium dry sherry; about one dozen roasted apples.

Pour 1 l of ale into a large pan. Add the sugar and cinnamon stick, and simmer the mixture slowly over low heat until the sugar has dissolved. Add the spices and lemon slices, the sherry and the remaining ale.

Twelfth Night Games

Because Twelfth Night is the last day of the Christmas festivities, it is particularly associated with parties and with games. Here are two for you to play:

Forfeit Song (from Marden, Herefordshire)

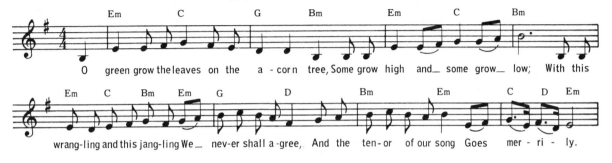

O green grow the leaves on the a - corn tree, Some grow high and__ some grow__ low; With this

wrang-ling and this jang-ling We__ nev-er shall a-gree, And the ten-or of our song Goes mer - ri - ly.

Twen - ty, nine-teen eigh-teen, sev-en-teen, six - teen, fif-teen, four-teen, thir-teen, twelve, e - lev- en, ten, nine,

eight, seven, six, five, four, three, two one, And the ten-or of our song Goes__ mer - ri - ly.

from *The Folklore of Herefordshire*, 1912, by E. M. Leather

Anyone singing this song, who missed a number or made a mistake, had to drink an extra glass of cider as a forfeit. What other forfeits could you suggest?

This puzzle was made up over 150 years ago. See if you can solve the questions? Can you make up a similar puzzle yourself?

Plough Monday

Up with your scrapers and down with your doors,
If you don't give us money we won't plough no more.

This rhyme was shouted by ploughmen, who used to go round the villages on Plough Monday – the first Monday after Twelfth Night. They would very often pull a plough decorated with ribbons. In some places they performed a mumming play. They also had songs. This one is called "Plough Monday".

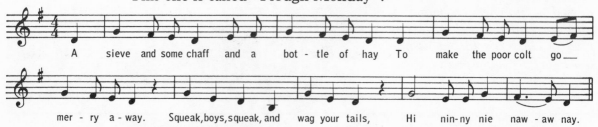

A sieve and some chaff and a bot-tle of hay To make the poor colt go — mer - ry a - way. Squeak, boys, squeak, and wag your tails, Hi nin-ny nie naw - aw nay.

Best accompanied with drone chord of G throughout, and rhythm provided (say) by guiro, rasp, claves and woodblock. Drone chord could be played as xylophone ostinato:

The "Hi" was bellowed as loudly as possible.

In some areas – Cambridgeshire, Leicestershire and Warwickshire, for example – this custom lasted until the 1920s or 30s. If you live in the country, you might like to ask any old people you know whether they remember it.

40

Candlemas

The Church introduced a Feast on 2 February to be held in honour of the Virgin Mary and the presentation of the infant Christ in the Temple at a time when Simeon had called him "A light to lighten the Gentiles". So, at the Feast of Candlemas, after the service had taken place, each of the worshippers took up one of the wax candles from the church and walked with it in procession through the town. During the Commonwealth period this practice was generally forbidden although it was still performed in some places. In 1628 there were complaints about the behaviour of the Bishop of Durham's chaplain, John Cozens, because he was continuing the traditional celebration:

On Candlemas Day last past, Mr Cozens, in renewing that popish ceremony of burning candles in honour of Our Lady, busied himself from two of the clock in the afternoon to four, in climbing long ladders to stick up wax candles in the said Cathedral Church. The number of all the Candles burnt that evening was two hundred and twenty, besides sixteen torches: sixty of those tapers and torches standing upon, and near, the High Altar (as he calls it), where no man came nigh.

from *Christmas to Candlemas*, 1931, by A. Bouquet

In the past, Candlemas, rather than Twelfth Night, was the final end of the Christmas celebrations when the decorations, especially the evergreens were taken down; winter was on the way out and spring was about to dawn. Hence this poem:

Ceremonies for Candlemas Eve

Down with the Rosemary and Bays,
　　Down with the Mistletoe;
Instead of Holly, now up-raise
　　The greener Box (for show).

The Holly hitherto did sway;
　　Let Box now domineer;
Until the dancing Easter-Day.
　　Or Easter's Eve appear.

Then youthful Box which now have grace,
　　Your houses to renew;
Grown old, surrender must his place,
　　Unto the crispèd Yew.

When Yew is out, then Birch comes in,
　　And many Flowers beside;
Both of a fresh, and fragrant kin
　　To honour Whitsuntide.

Green Rushes then, and sweetest Bents,
　　With cooler Oaken boughs;
Come in for comely ornaments,
　　To re-adorn the house,
Thus times do shift; each thing his turn does
　　　　　　　　　　　　　　　　hold;
New things succeed, as former things grow old.
Robert Herrick

Flowers in Winter

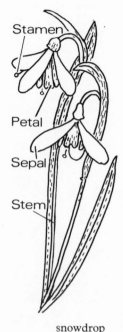

Stamen

Petal

Sepal

Stem

snowdrop

Winter is supposed to be the dead time for all flowers, but there are a few which can be seen, and they are the more valued because they come at this time of year. Some of them you might search for are :

> *January : snowdrop, aconite, Christmas rose*
> *February : lesser celandine, crocus*

Draw a picture of each, colour them carefully, and label the parts. Pick one sample of each flower you find, and press it, either between the pages of a big heavy book or, better, in a specially made flower press which you can easily buy. When the flower is pressed and dry, stick it neatly with sellotape into an exercise book or other album, and write the name, where you found it and the date you picked it, underneath. As the year goes on, pick more flowers, press them and stick them in your book, so that you compile your own book of pressed flowers.

A flower especially associated with Candlemas is the snowdrop, probably because of its resemblance to a candle and because it is one of the first flowers that brings us promise of spring. They are therefore sometimes known as "Mary's Tapers" or "Candlemas Bells".

St Valentine's Day

Valentine Chant

Good morn-ing to you, Val-en-tine, What you give me shall be mine. Rags be-hind and rags be-fore, Pray, old la-dy, re-mem-ber the poor. We're hard up, hard up, With-out food or fire, Have to lace our boots up With a lit-tle bit of wire.

from *Green Groves*, 1973, ed. by F. Hamer

Like so many of our festivals the Feast of St Valentine, 14 February, goes back at least to Roman origins. During the February festival that the Romans called Lupercalia, it was the custom for the young men to draw the names of young girls out of a box; whoever was chosen by chance in this way became their partner for the festival.

In his book, *The English Festivals*, Laurence Whistler gives this account of the first St Valentine's Day greetings telegram that his brother designed for the Post Office in 1935:

Copies of the gay-coloured form he designed, larger than usual and printed on better paper, were issued to every office of delivery, in advance. By the end of that day 49,000 had been despatched . . . in golden envelopes. The ordinary Greetings Telegram . . . had been introduced in 1935. By this time 15,000 of these were sent every week, or roughly 2,100 on any one day. Allowing that some of those handed in on February 14th were "ordinary greetings", this would seem to indicate that nearly 47,000 Valentines were claimed by the new method.

POST-OFFICE
Greetings Telegram

AMO
AMAS

Love in the present tense
Is perfect in its sense
Its future only good
In a conjunctive mood
Yet now with active voice
It prays you may rejoice

Dame Durden

Dame Durden kept five servant maids to carry the milking pail; She also kept five labouring men to use the spade and flail. 'Twas Moll and Bet and Doll and Kit and Dolly to drag her tail, It was Tom and Dick and Joe and Jack and Humphrey with his flail. Then Tom kissed Molly and Dick kissed Betty And Joe kissed Dolly and Jack kissed Kitty; And Humphrey with his flail, And Kitty she was the charming girl to carry the milking pail.

Dame Durden in the morn so soon she did begin to call;
To rouse her servant maids and men she did begin to bawl.

'Twas on the morn of Valentine when birds begin to prate;
Dame Durden and her maids and men they all together meet.

from *A Song for Every Season*, 1971, by Bob Copper

This song was popular at Harvest Home celebrations (see *Autumn*) in the south of England, though it was also sung in other parts of the country and at other times in the year. "Labouring men" are what we now call labourers; in this case, farm labourers. The flail (see illustration) was basically a stick which was used to beat the corn to thresh it, before machinery – in the shape of a threshing machine, and later the combine harvester – was invented to do the work.

Birds in Winter

The Parliament of Birds

One old tradition associated with St Valentine's Day was that it was the day on which the birds and the animals chose their mates for the coming year. A number of poems were written about this in the later middle ages, one of the best known being "The Parliament of Birds" by the English poet, Chaucer. Later John Donne wrote a love song to celebrate an actual marriage that had taken place on St Valentine's Day and used this old tradition of it being the day on which the birds were married. He imagines St Valentine as a Bishop conducting the marriage ceremonies:

> Hail Bishop Valentine, whose day this is,
>   All the air is thy diocese,
>   And all the chirping choristers
> And other birds are thy parishioners,
>   Thou marriest every year
> The lyric lark, and the grave whispering dove,
> The sparrow that neglects his life for love,
> The household bird, with the red stomacher,
>   Thou mak'st the blackbird speed as soon,
> As doth the goldfinch, or the halcyon;
> The husband cock looks out, and straight is sped,
> And meets his wife, which brings her feather-bed.
> This day more cheerfully than ever shine,
> This day, which might enflame thyself, old Valentine.

What do you think is the bird meant by the eighth line; and see if you can find what kind of bird is a "halcyon"?

You might like to do a drawing or painting of the ceremony of the birds turning up to be blessed by St Valentine.

Robin

The robin is specially remembered at Christmas. This is because postmen used to wear red coats and were called "Robins". When Christmas cards, brought by the postman, became common the robin seemed a good picture to have on a card.

The robin is actually a member of the thrush family. He seems a very friendly bird to us, because he is very curious. But to other birds he is often very spiteful. He has his own "territory" – it may be part of a garden, it may be several gardens – and he won't let other robins come there. This is probably to guard his own feeding ground.

A robin who invades another's territory will be attacked viciously. An invading robin is recognized by its red breast, and anything which seems like another robin – a bunch of red feathers, even, or a cock chaffinch with its pinky-red breast – may be attacked. Probably for this reason, young robins have yellowy breasts: if they had red breasts, other robins would attack them instantly before they learned to defend themselves.

Robins sing to proclaim their territory. Their song is clear and musical, though there is a high-pitched "tzee" and a sort of click in it in the mating season. Robins sing all the year round, and can often be heard at night as well as by day.

Robins eat worms and insects, and often build their nests in tin cans, on rubbish dumps or in sheds, as well as in trees or bushes. They lay about five eggs.

You could try observing a robin to try to discover how big his territory is, where it ends and how he defends it. Here is an imaginary map of robin's territories, to show a typical organization. See if you can draw a similar map of where you live.

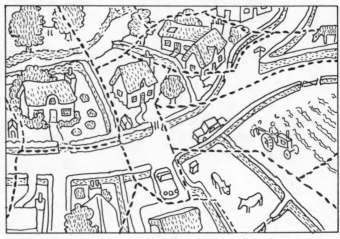

Imaginary map showing robins' territories

Chaffinch

The chaffinch is the commonest finch in Britain. Winter is the best time to see chaffinches, as they often fly about in flocks then. In summer they usually live in pairs.

The cock chaffinch is especially attractive, with a light blue crown, a brown mantle and a breast and throat which are almost red. The female has a dull green back. Both have white patches on their shoulders.

Notice the chaffinch's typical thick bill, adapted for eating seeds. In fact, because chaffinches eat the seeds of weeds, they are useful to have in the garden.

The chaffinch's nest is neat, made of moss, wool, hair, paper, and so on. It lays about five eggs, which are pale grey, speckled with red.

What other birds do you see in winter? Make a chart like this one of the birds you see :

Bird	Where seen	Colouring	Type of bill	Food	Nest	Eggs
Robin	Garden	Brown with red breast and white belly	Thin and pointed	Insects	In a shed	4–6

Try to draw the birds you see, colour them accurately, and label them.

Death of a Bird in January

It is on the grit of the road,
A dead starling, looking big,
With a blackish speckled body
And a beak like a long spike.
It is all beak and bony claws.

You exclaim from pity and stoop down,
Taking the bird very tenderly
In your gloved hand,
While our child pushes close.
She wants to feel and examine it,
She would pull it apart
From sheer exuberant curiosity,
Not cruel. You hold her off
And stand murmuring, rooted,
Asking if it is alive,
Grieving and staring down
And wrapping it in warm breath,
Until I have gone on, shouting:
"Let it rest in peace!"
For I think: All this tenderness
Is against nature, so why bother?
I am growing a tough skin
So as to live in this world.
I am a man. Stiff and churlish
I walk on, secretly moved.
You are generous without reason like a sun.

Philip Callow

The Bullfinch

I saw upon a winter's day
A bullfinch on a hedgerow spray;
He piped one note.
And since the countryside was mute,
As pure as rain I heard the flute
Of that small throat.

He picked a rotting willow-seed;
He whistled in his joy to feed,
A whole sweet stave.
His sloe-black head, how shining sleek,
How strong his blunted sooty beak,
His eye, how brave!

Then boldly down he came to drink
Out of a roadside puddle's brink,
Half ice, half mud;
So coral-breasted, sturdy, merry
That I forgave him plum and cherry
Nipped in the bud.

Betty Hughes

47

Pancakes and Shrovetide

Mix a pancake,
Stir a pancake,
Pop it in the pan;
Fry the pancake,
Toss the pancake –
Catch it if you can.

Chrisina Rossetti

Shrove Tuesday takes place between 2 February and 8 March depending upon the date of Easter. It is the last day before the beginning of Lent which is Ash Wednesday. On that day it was the custom to go to church to confess your sins and be absolved, or shriven. Because during Lent you were not allowed to eat fat, butter and eggs, the custom grew up of making pancakes on Shrove Tuesday so as to use up all the household stocks of these items.

Here is a traditional Welsh pancake recipe that you might like to try out for yourselves:

2 cups of flour
2 eggs
3 tablespoons melted butter
½ l milk
pinch of salt

First beat the eggs well. Pour the melted butter into the salt and flour, then add the eggs, beating well. Gradually pour in the milk, beating all the time so that the mixture is smooth. Leave to stand for about an hour, but beat up well again before using.

Lightly grease a heavy pan, and pour a tablespoon of the batter in when the pan is hot, tilting it so that the batter runs evenly over the pan. Let one side become golden, then turn and do the other side (you could try tossing them). You will know that the pancake is ready to turn when little bubbles come to the surface of the batter. You will find that this recipe makes about 20 pancakes, each 10 cm across. They can be eaten hot straight from the pan, or kept warm in a slow oven (about 130°C) until they are all ready.

The best way to serve them is with sugar and lemon juice squeezed on top of them, but some people like them with jam inside instead.

Traditionally in Wales pancakes were cooked on a bakestone, buttered whilst hot, piled one on top of another and then cut through into quarters. A very heavy frying pan will do instead of a bakestone.

Cân y Grempog (The Pancake Song)

Wraig y tŷ a'r teu - lu da, Os gwel-wch chi'n dda, ga'i grem - pog? Mae Mam rhy dlawd i
La - dy of this big, fine house, Please give me a pan - cake. Mam's too poor to

byrn - u blawd A 'Nhad rhy ddi - og i weith - io. Os gwel-wch chi'n dda ga'i grem - pog? Mae
buy an - y flour, And Dad's too la - zy to work, so, Please give me a pan - cake, I'm

'ngheg i'n grimp am grem - pog. Os nad oes men - yn yn y tŷ Rhowch lwy - ad fawr o dri - og. Ac os
dy - ing for a pan - cake. If you've no but - ter in the house, Give a spoon - ful of trea - cle, And

nad oes tri - og yn y tŷ Rhowch grem - pog fawr gyn - ddeir - iog, Gyn - ddeir - iog, gyn - ddeir - iog.
if you've no trea - cle in the house, Give me a great, big pan - cake, A pan - cake, a pan - cake.

from *Caneuon Llafar Gwlad*, Vol. 1, 1975, ed. by D. Roy Saer
translated by O. Griffiths and Roy Palmer

An extended chant, best sung unaccompanied. Different phrases could be sung by different soloists, or groups of singers. Unpitched percussion could be added.

In some parts of the country Shrove Tuesday (Pancake Day) is celebrated as a school holiday. Here is a 13-year-old-girl in Staffordshire writing about it:

My special day is Pancake Day, every child has a holiday.
Sometimes a fair comes to Longton and I think that everyone goes.
Some children make up rhymes about pancake day such as –

> Pancake Tuesday, mother's busy baking,
> We are helping, lovely pancakes making,
> Pancake Tuesday, mix them up and fry them,
> When they are done you can come and try them.

from *The Lore and Language of Schoolchildren* by I. and P. Opie

Do you know any traditional rhymes or customs in your part of the country connected with Pancake Day? Try asking your parents or grandparents to see if they can remember any. You might also be able to make up some pancake rhymes of your own on the lines of the ones quoted above.

Pancake Races

There are many old customs associated with Shrovetide. In some parts of the country people run Pancake Races. The one at Olney in Buckinghamshire is said to be more than five hundred years old. According to the story, in 1445 a woman from the village heard the bell calling her to church while she was making her pancakes. She ran to the church still wearing her apron and carrying her frying pan and this is how the tradition started.

Only women may take part in the race. The Pancake Bell is rung at 11.30 a.m. and again at 11.45 to warn contestants to get ready, and at 11.55 the race, which is over a 415-yard-long course, begins.

Each contestant has a frying-pan containing a pancake which is still cooking. She must toss the pancake three times during the race, which starts from the market square, and the first woman to reach the churchdoor and serve her pancake to the bellringer receives a kiss from him. She and the runner-up also receive a prayer book from the vicar. Those taking part must wear an apron and a hat or scarf.

There is also a pancake-tossing ceremony at Westminster School in London. At 11.00 a.m. a procession is led into the school and the school cook tosses a huge pancake over the 16-feet-high bar that separates the Upper from the Lower School. The boys all scramble for it and the one who gets the largest piece receives a cash prize which used to be a guinea. At one time all the boys in the school took part in the scramble but now there is just one representative from each form.

from *A Year of Festivals* by G. Palmer and N. Lloyd

The Pancake Race, Alcester

Frost

Frost occurs when the temperature of the ground or the air falls below the freezing-point of water (0°C). Frost is much more common in some places than others. For instance, Cornwall and Pembrokeshire have frost on only about ten days per year; over most of southern England, the average is between 25 and 50 days; but on high ground in northern England and Scotland, it occurs on average on over 100 days in the year.

Clear skies, light wind and dry air all favour frost. Can you find out why?

Here are the four basic kinds of frost:
Hoar frost: This is made up of dense white ice crystals, which often make beautiful feathery or spikey patterns.
Rime: This is a thin white layer of ice, usually found on the windward side of objects exposed to a cold, damp wind.
Silver thaw: This is a smooth transparent layer of ice, formed by a warm wet wind blowing over severely frozen ground.
Glazed frost: This is similar to silver thaw, a smooth transparent coating of ice on exposed surfaces. It is caused, however, by rain falling from a layer of warm air on to the frozen land. Both glazed frost and silver thaw are particularly dangerous on roads, being extremely slippery and not as noticeable as hoar frost and rime.

You might like to record on a weather chart the details of frost: how many times you have it, where it is thickest, what different sorts you experience, and so on.

Make Your Own Jack Frost Pictures

Frost on window panes is said to be painted by Jack Frost. You can make your own Jack Frost patterns by mixing a little thin paste with white poster paint, and brushing the mixture quite thickly over a sheet of coloured card. Then, with your finger nails, make patterns in the white paste: feathers, spikes, loops, twirls and fans.

Shrovetide Football

Football is the most famous game that seems to have had its origins at this time of the year. Here is a very early account of a Shrovetide football match:

On the day which is called Shrovetide, the boys of the respective schools bring each a fighting cock to their master, and the whole of that forenoon is spent by the boys in seeing their cocks fight in the schoolroom. After dinner, all the young men of the city go out into the fields to play at the well-known game of foot-ball. The scholars belonging to the several schools have each their ball; and the city tradesmen, according to their respective crafts, have theirs. The more aged men, the fathers of the players, and the wealthy citizens, come on horseback to see the contests of the young men, with whom, after their manner, they participate, their natural heat seeming to be aroused by the sight of so much agility, and by their participation in the amusements of unrestrained youth.

William Fitzstephen (died 1191)

Traditional football was played in the streets, or from end to end of the village at this time of the year for many centuries. There were hardly any rules – as many people as wanted to could usually play, and the goal might be something like the river at the end of the village. It was a rough game, hard and energetic, and often lasted all day.

Football at Kingston upon Thames, 1846

It was not until about 1850 that rules were laid down and regular competitions began, such as the F.A. Cup and, later, the Football League.

In March, 1888, William McGregor sent out a circular to the leading football clubs in the country, inviting them to send a representative to a meeting at Anderton's Hotel in Fleet Street, London. At the meeting, it was decided that a Football League should be started, and a month later, at another meeting at the Royal Hotel, Manchester, the Football League was officially formed, with twelve clubs participating. They were Accrington Stanley, Aston Villa, Blackburn Rovers, Bolton Wanderers, Burnley, Derby County, Everton, Notts County, Preston North End, Stoke City, West Bromwich Albion and Wolverhampton Wanderers. In the first season of the League, 1888–9, Preston North End easily won the Championship, with 40 points out of a possible 44 – 11 points ahead of Aston Villa, who were second. In 1892, a Second Division was added to the League, and later Third and Fourth Divisions.

There are now Football League clubs in practically every part of the country, and football is watched by more people than any other game. There is almost certainly at least one football club in your area, and you could trace its history and make a display about it. Follow the team's performances in the League and the F.A. Cup over the years, and read accounts of matches fifty or more years ago in your local newspaper, back copies of which are kept in the Library Archives. Who were the great players? What were the most exciting games? Visit the club's ground to see "behind the scenes" at a football club. Use pictures and the club colours to make the display bright and attractive. Write a letter to the local newspaper, appealing for memories, stories and souvenirs which will help to make the display more exciting.

Preston North End
Team, 1888–89

Traditional Games

It was about Shrovetide, too, that the spinning top season traditionally began in many areas, perhaps because with the coming of spring the ground was getting harder and drier and so tops would spin on it more easily. Here is one memory of what those days were like:

Oh those beautiful, delicate, boxwood tops, polished to a living gold, which we spun expertly from the hand . . . The . . . top was wound carefully with a cord, one end of which was licked to make it adhere to the stem of the top, and held at an angle in the right hand and with a quick throw and a backward jerk of the string was hurled at the pavement where it landed spinning with a quiet song, and . . . revolved on its motionless axis until its life was spent. . . . And the pavements, in the season, would be alive with tops: tiny, merry ones, large purring ones, coloured ones, wreathing a hay round one another.

from *The Boy Down Kitchener Street* by Leslie Paul

Whipping-top

Peg-top

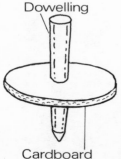

Dowelling

Cardboard

It is not always easy to get hold of proper spinning tops now and it takes a good deal of practice to make a top spin well. However, if you can get hold of one, or try to make one, you could hold top-spinning competitions to see who can manage it best.

It is, however, quite easy to make smaller and very attractive tops out of painted cardboard and a piece of dowelling. A top can be spun with the fingers, but a better result is usually obtained if you wind a piece of string round it and then pull the string sharply away, leaving the top spinning.

Marbles is another game that came into season at about this time of the year. There are lots of games that you can play with marbles. How many do you know? You might like to make a wall-chart showing the different games and their rules.

The marble season traditionally ended at the end of Lent on Good Friday when marbles championships were held and still are, for example at Tinsley Green in Sussex. There the game is played according to the rules of the British Marbles Control Board. A concrete ring, six feet across, is covered with sand. Each competitor in a team of six tries to knock out of the ring as many of the 49 marbles it contains as he can using his glass "tolley", a larger marble which he grips between forefinger and thumb and shoots without moving his whole hand. A variation on the game is to play it with only 13 marbles in the ring.

You can play the same game with a ring drawn on the ground or by throwing marbles into a hole scratched in the ground. Try organizing a marbles contest of your own.

Marbles

Talk with your parents or grandparents about the seasonal games they used to play when young. Make a list of these and give details of their rules and perhaps do some illustrations. You could make a booklet of seasonal games and pastimes. You might also be able to find some old children's playthings in a local museum.

Snow in the Suburbs

Every branch big with it,
Bent every twig with it;
Every fork like a white web-foot;
Every street and pavement mute:
Some flakes have lost their way, and grope back upward, when
Meeting those meandering down they turn and descend again.
The palings are glued together like a wall,
And there is no waft of wind with the fleecy fall.

A sparrow enters the tree,
Whereon immediately
A snow-lump thrice his own slight size
Descends on him and showers his head and eyes,
And overturns him,
And near inurns him,
And lights on a nether twig, when its brush
Starts off a volley of other lodging lumps with a rush.
The steps are a blanched slope,
Up which, with feeble hope,
A black cat comes, wide-eyed and thin;
And we take him in.

Thomas Hardy

Reference Section for Teachers

Books

Books of particular relevance to this volume are: *Christmas* by Kenyon Calthrop (Pergamon English Library); *Christmas Customs and Folklore* by Margaret Baker (Shire Publications); *Christmas Customs and Traditions* by Frank Muir (Sphere Books) and *The Penguin Book of Christmas Carols* ed. by Elizabeth Poston (Penguin).

Jackdaw No. 75, *Christmas*, (Jackdaw Publications Ltd) will be helpful in suggesting material for classroom display.

For mumming plays, see *Folk Plays* ed. by A. Adams and R. Leach (Harrap) and its companion volume, *The World of the Folk Play*.

A useful source of general reference about folk customs and practices is *Folklore, Myths and Legends of Britain*, published by the Reader's Digest Association. Geoffrey Palmer and Noel Lloyd's *A Year of Festivals* (Frederick Warne) is also a comprehensive guide to British calendar customs and is a useful library book. See also *The Country Life Book of Old English Customs* by Roy Christian (Country Life).

A number of the books in the "Discovering" series published by Shire Publications, Tring, Herts. are also useful, and we would especially recommend Margaret Gascoigne's *Discovering English Customs and Traditions*. There are numerous books dealing in detail with the folklore of different parts of the British Isles. The major publishing houses dealing in such matters include Batsford, David and Charles, E. P. Publishing, and Routledge and Kegan Paul. It is worthwhile consulting their catalogues to see if they have published any books dealing specifically with your own locality. Bob Copper's *A Song for Every Season* (Heinemann) will also be a valuable addition to the library resources. Other useful books are *The Jarrold Book of the Countryside in Winter* (Jarrold) and *Nature Through the Seasons* by Richard Adams and Max Hooper (Kestrel Books).

Records

Specially useful in connection with this volume are: *A Tapestry of Early Christmas Carols and Festive Music* (Music for Pleasure, CFP 177), and *Maypoles to Mistletoe* (Leader, LER 2092). The second record includes "The Seven Joys of Mary" and "A Waits Carol" as well as some other traditional material (though not everything on this record is traditional).

The major folk song record company is Topic Records of 27 Nassington Road, London NW3 2TX. Their complete catalogue is well worth having, especially as it lists several collections of local folk songs belonging to particular areas of the British Isles. We would especially recommend the Watersons' records, *Frost and Fire* (12T 136), *Songs of Ceremony* (12T 197), and *For Pence and Spicy Ale* (12TS 265). It should, however, be noted that the latter record consists of field recordings of elderly singers, and may not always be easy to use with younger pupils. The same applies to another Topic record, *Animal Songs* (12T 198). There is also a record (LED 2067) based on the book, *A Song for Every Season,* produced by Leader Records, 209 Rochdale Road, Halifax, Yorks., HX4 8SE.

Museums and Libraries

There are an increasing number of museums with local folklore collections and also several local specialist folk museums. Full details of all these will be found in the annual A.B.C. Publication, *A Guide to Museums and Art Galleries in Great Britain,* which is a very helpful source of information.

Most libraries also have a local collection of great interest.

Organizations

The following national organizations can provide much help and information:

The English Folk Dance and Song Society whose headquarters are at Cecil Sharp House, 2 Regent's Park Road, London NW1 7AY. The Society publishes an annual Folk Directory which gives up-to-date information about folk-customs, and there is also the Ralph Vaughan Williams Memorial Library at Cecil Sharp House itself. This includes a useful picture collection.

The Folklore Society, c/o University College, Gower Street, London WC1E 6BT, can also provide help and information.

In addition, there are numerous local history and archeological societies that can provide speakers or mount exhibitions in schools. Many of these produce local publications of great value for teaching purposes.